Since a series of spiritual encounters began in 2014, Prudence Audrey Assogba has uncovered hidden truths including the reality of reincarnation and the existence of elves and angels. But most tangibly, she befriended a legendary winged horse – actually an elfic spiritual being – lacking explanation in common knowledge. Given the lack of accurate information about this mystical 'winged mare' coupled with the profound first-hand experiences between woman and creature, Prudence chose to disclose their encounters within these pages. Her account bridges understanding around the winged horse's origins while filling a literary void. Expanding beyond to broader topics, Prudence also chronicles pivotal moments from her spiritual journey. Through relatable stories and otherworldly happenings alike, she makes the extraordinary accessible.

This book is dedicated to all truth seekers and to those who, as referred to by the Lord Jesus, have remained children at heart.

Prudence Audrey Assogba

THE WINGED MARE EXPLAINED AND SIGNS OF SPIRITUAL ASCENSION

AUSTIN MACAULEY PUBLISHERS™
LONDON * CAMBRIDGE * NEW YORK * SHARJAH

Copyright © Prudence Audrey Assogba 2024

The right of Prudence Audrey Assogba to be identified as author of this work has been asserted by the author in accordance with sections 77 and 78 of the Copyright, Designs and Patents Act 1988.

All rights reserved. No part of this publication may be reproduced, stored in a retrieval system, or transmitted in any form or by any means, electronic, mechanical, photocopying, recording, or otherwise, without the prior permission of the publishers.

Any person who commits any unauthorised act in relation to this publication may be liable to criminal prosecution and civil claims for damages.

A CIP catalogue record for this title is available from the British Library.

ISBN 9781035822423 (Paperback)
ISBN 9781035822430 (ePub e-book)

www.austinmacauley.com

First Published 2024
Austin Macauley Publishers Ltd®
1 Canada Square
Canary Wharf
London
E14 5AA

I am sending out my sincerest thanks to all the people who made it possible for this book to reach publication.

Table of Contents

Foreword	11
What the Winged Mare Truly Is	12
How to Receive the Entity or What Creates the Connection	13
The Personality of Pegasus	14
How the Reception Takes Place	15
What the Reception Brings to the Person	17
What Else to Ask or to Obtain from This Entity	18
How to Maintain Connection with the Winged Mare or How to Avoid Losing the Connection	19
A Personal Encounter with Pegasus	20
The Symbolism of the White Horse and How It Manifests Itself	22
Spiritual Ascension: Some of the Signs Based on a Personal Journey	24
End Word	53

Foreword

It is my prayer that the greatest number possible of people reach the state of grace of a winged mare, the state of a human being who is free in their mind and receives spiritual guidance directly in their soul.

To those who are going through the symptoms of spiritual ascension and might not understand what is happening to them, I hope this book will bring some enlightenment and some comfort through the realisation that they are not alone.

This book is dedicated to all truth seekers and to those who, as referred to by the Lord Jesus, have remained children at heart.

What the Winged Mare Truly Is

This message was received through contact with the Winged Mare itself along with the chief of nature's beings called elves. The Holy Spirit was present at each discussion session. Many stories have been written about Pegasus. No one has said who Pegasus truly is.

The Winged Mare is not a doctrine but rather a spiritual concept.

The Winged Mare is a hermaphrodite spiritual entity that comes inside of a person when the latter reaches a certain level of goodness and spiritual enlightenment.

Some people connect to it through witchcraft, but then it does not stay. Most of the people called upon its reception should have it through Christianity.

The Winged Mare itself, the horse, which is called Pegasus in Greek mythology, exists spiritually as an elfin creature who lives in the darkest parts of forests, lakes, villages, cemeteries, and bushes.

The entity also resides around beaches and some ancient sites, such as the Northern Ontario area, deserts, the Grand Canyon, etc. This being manifests itself as a male entity to female friends and as a female entity to male friends.

How to Receive the Entity or What Creates the Connection

Kindness rooted in selfless service and generosity leads to the reception of this entity but, truly, attachment to Christian values in general (regardless of whether someone goes to church or not) should create this connection in the near future.

Another way of obtaining this reception is to mature in spiritual knowledge or rituals, or through constantly repeated prayers.

One more way to obtain this grace is to demonstrate kindness towards others through biblical teachings, and conferences on various subjects, whether of a religious or spiritual nature or not.

The Personality of Pegasus

Pegasus is a solitary entity who prefers not to visit people or be in a crowd too often. This is a very serious entity that does not allow playing around with spiritual matters or fornicating with just about anybody in a disproportionate manner. Most sexual games are allowed, provided that they are conducted with a given or proven partner.

The main traits are as follows:

- Very serious about life in general
- Likes to joke around with people but also test them out sometimes in manners that are not always funny
- Likes to eat comfortably and thus appreciates a receiver who is a food lover
- Likes to play a little from time to time
- Appreciates gratefulness
- Laughs at itself sometimes
- Hates witchcraft
- Hates being disrespected

How the Reception Takes Place

This happens in a tangible, very physical manner. The entity enters your womb or your head directly.

One day, the person will feel a presence in their body and then hear a voice in their head or within them telling them: "I am the Winged Mare. I am with you" or "I am here to put some order in your life" or "I am here to help you accomplish certain things".

The spirit will ask the person how they want to be in life or to what kind of purpose they want to destine their life. This is a life force that manifests itself rarely to people in nature as an elf or elfin creature: a human being of a very petite size (such as the height of a tree shoot) with very long hair.

When you encounter one physically, instead of spiritually, you close your eyes and wait for any instruction or guidance from the entity. Closing one's eyes is meant to avoid the dematerialisation of your body upon death, meaning the complete disappearance of the body.

When people go to some of the places above mentioned, they should start praying that the entity manifests itself. But in general, they should just wait around and the entity will come inside of them. It could ask them not to look at a specific area where the entity could be standing.

If the connection does not take place on a given day, it could happen magically at a different moment, even in the person's place of residence. In this latter instance, they might even be prompted to simply go outside of their living space, perhaps to the garden or the front door, and the entity will manifest there through some spiritual portal mysteriously.

A person who receives this spiritual entity is called a winged mare.

What the Reception Brings to the Person

Mainly quicker or quick obtention of anything that the person wants in life. Generally speaking, Pegasus brings inspiration in many various fields to different kinds of people. The Winged Mare is good at:

- Fulfilling life promises faster
- Making living more enjoyable: he or she brings the feeling that life is worth living and there are things to hope for, no matter how little or big one's life promises are, no matter the social rank or status of the person who is receiving it
- Bringing spiritual knowledge to a specific area
- Bringing spiritual stamina or strength in certain areas or in all areas according to the person's life path or personal spiritual journey
- A rekindling of hope through special connections or renewal of great relationships, whether one or several, created or improved in a magical manner
- Increasing life's gifts that the person already has
- Making the person want to be free to be themself.

What Else to Ask or to Obtain from This Entity

This is a spirit of divination as well. One could ask questions about anything of a preoccupying nature for the person. From the most superficial subjects to the most serious matters.

How to Maintain Connection with the Winged Mare or How to Avoid Losing the Connection

The Winged Mare does not like uncontrolled fornication, as mentioned previously. Sexual relationships in a disorderly manner are prohibited. The entity will come and go in one's life in general, but it disappears completely when it realises that the person is too playful with sexual matters, or that the connection has been established through witchcraft.

Therefore, it goes into a state of dormancy within the person or entity until they reach a state of pure spiritual knowledge or power.

However, it is necessary to specify that the Winged Mare goes often into dormancy even when there is harmony with the person who receives it. The spirit must be in that state for life promises or the desired living conditions to unfold almost mysteriously.

The person who receives it must maintain a lot of purity in their intentions. Their heart must be shaped or clothed in white, so to speak. The Winged Mare leaves the person's body completely if they do not maintain some cleanliness in their surroundings.

A Personal Encounter with Pegasus

Elves are real. They do exist and I have known this for a fact since I became a winged mare. My encounter with Pegasus took place in two stages.

One fine morning in August, I heard the voice of Christ asking me to go outside immediately. As I went near the lawn on the side of the apartment complex, I felt a presence in my back. I was then asked to go back inside my apartment. When I did this, I heard some male voice telling me that he was the chief of elves and he would be helping me heal from some mental issues to which I was subjected for quite a while.

He explained how his manifestation must be spiritual essentially and said that before any collaboration could take place, he had to access my mind in order to read into my akashic record and assess the state of my soul. I allowed the investigation as my intentions are always clean, and when he finished the investigation, he expressed deep compassion for all the abuses, the violence, and the treasons of which I have been a victim. He also mentioned that he either brings more trouble or helps soothe, depending on whether he deems the person to be of a good or bad character.

He then promised to help me reach financial stability as well as mental repose, for I have been striving so hard to make ends meet and I had gone through several spiritual and psychological attacks.

He also referred to the fact that he would be departing from my body from time to time to return to the bush, where he truly resides.

Over the course of our interactions, a few weeks later, another elfin creature accessed my physical body and named himself as the Winged Mare. A dialogue started with the latter, leading to the actual confirmation that the elf is a real spiritual entity who can manifest itself to the naked eyes as well on extremely rare occasions.

Both entities were able to communicate with me in every language that I spoke to them.

The Symbolism of the White Horse and How It Manifests Itself

This elfin creature named Pegasus is a tiny spiritual human being whose soul resides sometimes inside a mystical horse of pure white colour. When the entity is about to introduce itself to a chosen person, this person receives, during nighttime, the holographic image of a pure white horse approaching him or her. The horse really has two wings.

The white colour symbolises the purity of intentions so dear to this entity and the peacefulness that Pegasus intends to bring to the person. It also entails the courage to live by one's own values, the freedom gained from this choice, and the freedom to roam around the world.

Another reason for the white colour is that it represents independence of thought as well as endurance in the face of life's struggles; hence, the ability to run the extra mile.

MOMENTS AROUND WHICH SPIRITUAL DOORS OPEN AND CLOSE

The opening and closing of spiritual doors may range from a few hours to the entire day, and even several days in a row.

Some spiritual doors open during nighttime around the hours of 8 p.m. or 10 p.m.

They can also open during the early hours of the day around 3 a.m.

Those doors may close around 12 a.m., 5 a.m., or 6 p.m.

Some other spiritual doors open around the hours of 9 a.m., 10 a.m. 11 a.m., and 12 p.m.

The latter may close around 12 a.m., 1 p.m., 2 p.m., 3 p.m., 5 p.m., 7 p.m., or 9 p.m.

However, during this special epoch in which we are living, all sorts of spiritual doors may open and close at any time of the day, depending on the life path or the type of experiment to which the awakened person is subjected.

Spiritual Ascension: Some of the Signs Based on a Personal Journey

Before a person can see the white horse, their spiritual eye, also referred to as the third eye, must be opened. This opening of the third eye comes in different ways to different people. Personally, as someone whose life path is that of a spiritual master, the journey started upon the death of my mother and spanned over several years. I am aware that the type of spiritual awakening that I have been through is or will be experimented on by some other people. I am therefore sharing here this experience in order to help those who, like me, might have strange visions or strange bodily reactions so that they know that they are not alone on this path.

The goal of the spiritual awakening, also called kundalini awakening in Buddhism, is to guide us towards healthier ways of doing things, not to lead us to live in an imaginary world while the world around us is collapsing. I say this because, through the infiltration of the New Age movement, there is another ongoing work of diversion of souls who are made to believe that everything is perfect as it is. I have already heard crazy things such as oppressed people are souls who chose to sacrifice themselves to allow the rest of the world to progress, or that one should not pay too much attention to everything happening in order to remain focused on seeking the light. Yet, the purpose of awakening is not to escape the physical reality, it is rather to see it in all its nakedness; to have one's eyes wide open on what is going on and to encourage others to do the same, which does not mean either to force them to follow the same path as oneself, but to draw their attention to the abnormalities. Once one has discovered the existence of a parallel reality, it is recommended to get out of that cosy cocoon and come back down to Earth to express in it this new consciousness unfolding. We want to improve life in this world, not flee towards another plane of existence. To awaken does not consist either in following some sort of new trend, but very much in adopting some behaviours and a way of living that is healthier and that way, setting an example around us. To access the light does not mean to see life through rose-coloured glasses, but to see things as they really are – both the beauty of the world and its ugliness – and to choose to live or work in a way to help reduce the ugly things noted.

In Africa and in the diaspora, it is rather false priests and false pastors who are busy exploiting people's spiritual thirst by doing commerce on the back of God. We must be careful about where we set our feet because their goal is to sow confusion in our minds in order to better exploit us.

As our thoughts can materialise faster than before, we will have to be careful with what we think about and the words that come out of our mouths. We must then make sure to mean what we wish for and what we say.

As our vibration gets higher and higher, our knowledge becomes more and more empirical. Sometimes, you simply "know" something, without even having the proof of it. When you start seeing the abnormality in certain social rules and you realise that finally there is some sanity in your being different, there will be an upheaval in your habits. Do not reject yourself, do not judge yourself. This is a natural process and a state of grace. You have started being born again. Be grateful for that, for it is the beginning of a journey towards serenity. Also, know that it is a process that takes time. Depending on each person's efforts and path, it can last months or years, in reality, this is a life-long quest. But because we are living in very special times, it will be accelerated for many through the people who receive the power to baptise with the Holy Spirit. Nonetheless, we will have to put all impatience aside and just focus on our life-learning process while listening carefully to ourselves and to the messengers that the universe is sending to guide us. The less one seeks to run, the faster one progresses in this field. It is a personal transformation that you have no obligation to discuss until you feel that the time is right to do so. The reason for listing some signs for you is to avoid panicking when your body manifests certain reactions and to allow you to recognise them for what they really are: a blessing. If you feel the need to discuss it, do so with people with whom you feel open about the subject or who are on the same path. If you discuss it with people who choose to remain blind, their words will only make you more depressed than necessary or bring you to panic. If at some point you feel really ill, you should of course seek treatment, but if it is your nature to see a doctor when you have the slightest discomfort, you risk disturbing your spiritual ascension by subjecting yourself to treatments for something that is not a pathology. Many people incarnated with a spiritual mission have thus slowed down their awakening by letting fear or material concerns take control over them. Fear is a natural feeling. However, when it sets in, we must make a great effort so as not to let it take over. Often, imagining the worst-case scenario or invoking the assistance of God, of Christ, or of a saint, such as the archangel Saint Michael, guardian of our souls' salvation, can help. You will know that you are moving in the right direction in your spiritual quest when the signs that I am about to enumerate start manifesting for you. The symptoms may vary per individual and the following list is not exhaustive. Inevitably, however, you will identify for the most part with the following description.

The elevation takes place in three stages. The first phase, which represents the longest one and can finish after a few years or last a lifetime, is the most painful. It consists of cleaning the emotional, spiritual, and mental baggage related to individual karma. The second phase consists of an increased awareness of social scourges, which results in constant questioning about collective issues at the local and global levels. The person is in constant observation about his environment and his own relationship with this environment; his understanding of the process of life increases. His look is more critical concerning the gap between what should be and what is, but his level of tolerance towards human weaknesses increases simultaneously. He judges less and less and paradoxically, he is less accepting of bad behaviours and unwilling to make efforts for improvement; probably because he realises that improvement is possible after having experimented with it himself. At this stage, the self loses its importance, one sees oneself as a tiny part of a big whole. The third phase is the one where absolute serenity is reached. The person is no longer dependent at all on how others see him or their opinion about him while learning to take the utmost account of different views. At the same time, the ability to distinguish between what is right and what is erroneous improves, helping to better appreciate various opinions. The understanding of life deepens even more. On one hand, one realises that we cannot finish learning and accepts this fact, and on the other hand, one learns to maintain inner peace under all circumstances. The upheavals will occur at the psychological, emotional, and physical levels.

Psychological and Emotional Upheavals

RELATIONAL CHANGES: Overnight, you no longer accept some situations or behaviours that you could bear previously. You have the impression of being stricter towards certain behaviours and more allergic than ever to negativity. Yet, paradoxically, you feel more compassionate and you find it more easy to be tolerant. Distance occurs between you and some people you have socialised with for years and despite your goodwill, the gap grows. Certain long-time relationships break apart for one reason or another. You start questioning things that seemed normal to you up to that point. You start remembering events from the past with a deeper understanding of their meaning.

PAINFUL EXPERIENCES: You have recently experienced or will experience some tragic event that not only shakes you but also causes deep reflections in you. It can be the sudden death of a loved one, sometimes several deaths, it can be an accident or a serious illness, a painful job loss, the breaking up of a long-time friendship or love relationship, or even an accumulation of painful events during the same period, which was my own case.

SUDDEN MOOD CHANGES: An intense emotional upheaval made of moments of deep sadness and tears, because the negative karma must be washed away. Personal sensation of the suffering of the world or depression. Sometimes, profound doubt about the existence of God, which can be brief or prolonged for years, depending on each person's background. This stage, which is necessary, is called, "the dark night of the soul", by the Spanish mystic John of the Cross. It will also happen that you feel the deepest joys and be enthusiastic about things as simple as the fact as breathing, a shared smile, a greeting from a stranger in the street, or the weather, regardless of whether it is raining, snowing, windy, etc., and be absolutely certain that God is with you.

INCREASING NUMBER OF SYNCHRONICITIES: *Coincidences* multiply in your life. You meet new people who share the same interests or whose acquaintances bring new elements to your vision of things. You are actually attracting them towards you; this is the law of attraction at play. You ask yourself a question and the answer comes to you through a song, a movie, somebody's words, an article in the newspaper, etc. You *bump into* the answer so to speak. Sometimes, if following some reflection you come to a certain conclusion, it is possible that right away you find a coin, often placed right in front of you, at times placed at the most unusual place. Pick it up and thank angels for their benevolent presence. It is a way for your guardian angel or your spiritual guides to approve your conclusion or to signal to you their protection or their support if it was rather some feeling that you were having at that specific moment. It has already happened to me, to see the silhouette of the angel and to see the coin appear right away beside me while I was at work and had not left any coin on my desk. If you start finding paper clips, sometimes at unusual places, repeatedly, it is a message from God to remind you of his constant presence. It is a symbol of unity (that which holds two or several things together), of life (the circular shape of the paper clip), and of attachment (it means we are always together). It may be to notify you and reassure you about upcoming changes about which you might otherwise worry. Thus, a short while after, I grasped the meaning of this repeated sign, some movements started inside my brain, as if paths were being traced in it. You know our DNA is like a computer program. At some stage during the ascension, the kundalini will start in a certain way to reprogram you depending on the level at which your soul is in its journey. You will sense a perfect logic in this work that is being carried out in your body and it can be frightening if you are not notified about what is happening. Each time I had bizarre sensations, I thought about the paper clip message: "I am with you, no need to worry."

INCREASING NEED FOR SOLITUBE: You increasingly feel the need to spend some time alone, even if you still love to socialise. You simply feel the need to be less in groups in order to spend more time doing introspection. Without isolating yourself, it is necessary to find some time for yourself, for it is in the silence and the calm that you will perceive the secrets of your soul. You will also feel the need to slow down in your activities.

INCREASING NEED FOR AUTHENTICITY: You can no longer play the "make-believe" game. Like a child, when you disapprove of something, you let it be known. Conversely, you express your approval with sincerity and you marvel at little things. Jesus said beforehand that we would discover the kingdom of heaven only by becoming like children again. Several authors reflected upon the question of the inner child if you are interested in learning more about it. Simply, you lose all malice, your intentions are never double, and you learn again to appreciate the small gifts from life. You are no longer easy to manipulate. When someone is deceiving you, you know it instinctively, but you avoid judging, conscious that that person is acting based on their understanding of the moment and confident that one day, he or she will overcome such a way of doing if he or she is willing to improve. For you yourself are the evidence that it is possible to make improvements when one is willing. You clearly see that your own way of being, thinking, and doing things is evolving. You distinctively see the old you, the new one, and the possibilities of progress that are left. You feel changes in the environment and you increasingly feel the need to be in contact with nature, to find some time just to empty your mind and appreciate the silence.

Physical Upheavals

EXTREME FATIGUE: You experience massive periods of lack of energy without apparent reason. This is normal because the purification requires from your body an enormous use of energy that you cannot see. Additionally, you will develop a heightened sensitivity to the vibrations circulating in the places to which you go. Each time my body craves some rest, I drop everything. I sometimes spend an entire day doing nothing but relaxing when it is possible. Once my energy is renewed, I am able to work efficiently for several days in a row. The only real spiritual exercise that I do is to offer myself some moments of complete silence and stillness, ranging from one to several hours. At least once per day, when I wake up, I also pay attention to my breathing, I breathe in and breathe out slowly and deeply for a few minutes. I take that opportunity to say a little inner prayer to thank God for waking me up, to put the day ahead under his protection and to ask for the advent of a new era of love, peace and shared abundance. When I go to bed, I say again a little inner thank-you prayer no matter how the day has been. My prayers are always like a dialogue rather than a simple formality. It is like when you tell a close person about your day and you express your gratitude for having that person by your side. No matter what your method is, the important thing is to avoid developing some ritual in your way of communicating with God. In fact, when you are talking to yourself in your head all day long, you are having a conversation with God. Praying efficiently is just a matter of being conscious that God is there, in your head and heart, and consciously addressing your thoughts to Him. It is a matter of not treating Him like a stranger for He is the best friend and the most understanding friend you can ever have.

SLEEP DISTURBANCES: At certain times, one has the impression of not getting enough sleep, and there is frequent insomnia; at other times, your sleep will be very deep and restful even if it is of short duration. Some episodes of sleep paralysis can be experienced as well.

INCREASE IN THE FREQUENCY OF DREAMS: You dream more often than before and some of your dreams are lucid, which means that during the dream you are conscious that you are dreaming. If you want, you can find a good book on dream interpretation to help you get a general idea about the symbols that appear in your dreams, as well as the meaning of colours and numbers. The book cannot give you the meaning of your dreams, but through the symbolism, it can bring you some ideas to guide you. You dissect each symbol separately, then you establish a link between the different scenes while trying to place them into the context of the things that are happening in your life during that time. The details are often very important in a dream. For example, if you see a cloth, pay attention to the colour and quality of the fabric, pay attention to the time of the day or to the hour appearing in the dream, if there are doors, notice whether they are open or closed, etc. Over time, you will become familiar with some symbols and you will be able to do some interpretations without any tool. You can also pray that the meaning be revealed to you. Some dreams will be so clear that you will understand them instantly. Sometimes, you are warned through dreams of a present or upcoming situation to give you a chance to act for the best, and positively change some negative fate whenever possible. Some other times, you will understand the meaning of your dreams only when the events are unfolding or after they have occurred. If you forget a dream upon awakening, do not force your memory to reconstitute it. The important details will always come back to your mind or will be reminded to you by your Higher Self one way or the other. If you can afford to do so, one good method consists of simply remaining in a lying position a little longer, asking God to remind you of the important details, and waiting to see if the dream comes back partially or totally. If it does, that's good, if it does not, that's fine too. It can also happen that you have premonitory dreams even if you never had any before. Dreams are a powerful means of communication between the spiritual world and the material world. There are three kinds of them: real dreams, chimeric dreams, and interference dreams.

- **Chimeric dreams** are constructions of our own mind which send back to us some images of our psychological state of the moment: it is a reflection of our thoughts and emotions of the moment, of our fears, or even of the pain related to some disease or suffering. They are therefore not real.
- **Interference dreams** are images transmitted to our minds by some negative entities. They can be frightening images, scenes of inappropriate, or even perverse, desires or actions, suggested by malevolent spirits to mislead us or to fuel confusion in our mind and attract us towards the path of illusions. These types of dreams can be caused by some people or beings who want to harm us personally, in which case they are called spiritual attacks. They can also be caused by the simple fact that we happen to be in a geographic location crossed by some negative energy to which we end up being temporarily exposed. If during such a dream I really feel threatened, I always call Jesus to help me. If I wake up with the strange feeling that there really is an attack on my person, I say, either out loud, either mentally, depending on the

situation, that I do not authorise any negative entity around me and that if any evil spirit persists in persecuting me, he be burned by the blood of Jesus. In fact, a soul that is evolving spiritually will necessarily enter into contact with the dark parts of the spiritual realm at some point. Even if you make every effort to avoid evil spirits, they will know how to find you for their goal is to prevent as many people as possible from ascending in order for them to keep reigning here below. On several occasions at the beginning of my spiritual awakening, it happened that I found myself fighting in my bed while I was half awake or I felt with my eyes wide open, one or several presences trapping my arms and legs as though they were trying to tie me up, or even that I feel a hand trying to either suffocate me or drag me violently out of the bed. Each time that I could, I wrestled. When I felt totally powerless, I silently invoked the Lord Jesus, I told him that I had no strength and asked him to come to my rescue and that if anything happened to me, I was asking that he render justice to me. Very quickly, I felt freed and I regained peace. Gradually, not only such experiences decreased, but more frequently, I was able to have the upper hand whether it was in a full dream or in a half-awakened state; it seems that the simple fact of saying Jesus gives me some sudden strength.

- As for **real dreams**, they appear in the form of a clear vision of an upcoming event or one that has already occurred (in the second case the goal is to explain it to us), or even of an ongoing situation. They can come from God himself or from benevolent spirits to warn us about some danger, to transmit some information or teaching, to encourage or advise us, or simply to speak with us as one does with physical persons. On several occasions, some benevolent spirits who transmitted some important message to me in dreams woke me up so that by seeing them I realised that the message was important. Generally, when you have had a real dream, you know it because the feeling is strong, even if you do not remember the details of it when you wake up. If the message is very important, as long as you remain still a moment after awakening, God himself sends us the images back and gives us their meaning intuitively. It already happened that I forget the details of a dream, but the simple fact of pondering about the meaning of one or several symbols that appeared in it brings all the rest of it to my memory. On several occasions also I had dreams which were not revelations, but what I would call conversations on some situation by which I was preoccupied. It is always comforting to know that there are some people we do not see who care about our well-being. On one occasion, I received an invitation that I intended to decline. But on the day preceding the day I wanted to send my response, I had that dream in which I saw myself at the event seated at a specific spot and manifestly pleased that I went. So, I understood that I had to accept the invitation. I thus went to the event and I even made sure to put on the outfit that I saw myself wearing in the dream. It so happened that I was re-gathered there with someone who is dear to me and the evening turned out to be a nice and relaxing moment during a period where I did not really have my mind on partying.

NIGHT SWEATS AND FLUCTUATIONS OF BODY TEMPERATURE: You sometimes wake up with your clothes wet because you sweated abundantly on your whole body while you were sleeping. It can happen that you feel lighter after these nocturnal sweats which will manifest for a short length of time. They occur when you receive new cosmic energy and some of your old energy is washed away. Due to the differences in temperature between the energy coming from the cosmos and your body, you will have an increased sensitivity to cold weather. Sometimes, you will feel cold even if the weather is very warm and a few moments later you could feel very hot. It will be up to you to see, depending on what goes on in your body, how to adapt your clothing to these changes.

VARIOUS CONVULSIONS: Sometimes your body is shaken by jerking movements or you jump in your sleep or even while you are awake. Do not worry, you are not sick. And this does not mean that your spiritual awakening is going wrong or that some demonic force is taking over your body. For certain, there is more pain when one opposes resistance to the process, but you are simply undergoing an internal transformation through a gust of new energy which will break through all the energy blockages in you. From my experience, the intensity decreases gradually over time. I have also noticed that on days that I have important obligations to fulfil or that I am very busy at work, the divine spirit makes accommodations for me by reducing the sensations completely, and then resuming when I am alone or in bed. One day, I was precisely granted one of these accommodations to go complete some administrative formality and after my errand, I decided impulsively to go wandering in a shopping centre, the symptoms came back so brutally that I understood that I was being strongly advised against this distraction when indeed I had other important things to do that day. I started laughing and, my eyes closed, I told the Lord: "It is true that you read all my thoughts. And it is true that this is not the day to be wasting time. I will wisely go home and dissect those documents." Instantaneously, I regained *peace* with the time to go home. This is good proof that the strength of the symptoms is normality that can vary per individual and that they are being attenuated for us to the extent possible.

You might happen to feel like electricity is running through your entire body and the body might be subject to frequent jolts, as though you were receiving electric shocks. Many times, these abrupt movements over which I had no control kept me awake all night, at times continuing throughout the day, exhausting me physically. What happens in this instance is not due to muscle contractions such as in the case of spasms. One clearly feels the travelling of the energy in the body and it is a more or less violent, rapid movement that causes the convulsions. After a series of *shocks*, I literally feel some light floating on my skull sometimes.

SENSORY DISTURBANCES: Depending on your own physical constitution and your nature, some of your senses will sharpen or worsen temporarily. If it is the hearing, for example, which will be the case for the majority of people, you will become more receptive to the soft rustle of silence; at times, you will feel ringing in the ears, which will decrease in intensity until it stops at some point. If you concentrate on it each time the phenomenon occurs, you will be able to perceive much more subtle sounds that will procure you a sense of gentle tranquillity. The eyesight can also be affected, by a heightened perception of colours, visions of light while the eyes are closed, etc.

ANGELS SIGHTING OR SIGNS OF ANGELIC PRESENCE: After some time, you will start seeing flashes of blue or white light, or some other colour, appearing at certain moments as though to approve the sentence you just pronounced, the encounter you just had, the place you are visiting, etc. Progressively, these flashes of light will start moving, you will perceive shapes; it is in reality, the movement of angels or spiritual guides circulating around you. Sometimes, their presence is signalled by a sweet floral fragrance. Occasionally, they can manifest their presence through a tiny feather dancing or moving in front of you, or even in the form of sparks of light passing as though they were winking at you. This game will sometimes make you laugh or smile, which would be the result they were seeking at that moment to let you know that you are loved and valued by them. Thank them mentally and express your gratitude, or whatever you feel, in return.

They can also send you messages through a series of numbers of the same value, such as a succession of 1 or 2, etc. Depending on the circumstances, this will be to warn you against some danger, to confirm their protection, or to tell you what cycle of transformation you are engaging in, etc. On rare occasions, they can take on a human form to come and give you some advice directly. Be careful not to discourage such a precious intervention. If God or an angel wants to meet you in a physical form, he can, out of infinite wisdom, take on the appearance with which you will feel more comfortable, but there is a strong probability that they appear like a very modest person, sometimes an eccentric one, or even like a mad person or a beggar, in short, like one of those people to whom not much importance is given or that are generally kept at bay. We should therefore avoid looking at people with contempt. But while keeping our politeness, we must be careful to not give our trust too easily because there is a lot of deception in the physical world. That is why we must develop our instincts. Animals in nature do not have the luxury to decipher behaviours and words, they thus let their intuition guide them enormously. You will not be able to make friends with everybody, unfortunately.

We are all born with a guardian angel assigned by God who follows us permanently during our whole life; he is one of those who never entered the material world. He accompanies us and guides us when we are willing to pay attention to his signs. Along the way, based on our choices and the types of help that we request, we receive additionally, some more or less punctual help from a varying number of protective spirits or spiritual guides who can be other angels, deceased parents, or some ascended souls who for various reasons decide to assist us.

UPHEAVAL OF DIETARY HABITS, THE ISSUE OF VEGETARIANISM: There will be some periods of big appetites followed by periods of total loss of appetite that will seem like some sort of natural fast lasting for one or several days. On those days, it can happen that your body rejects even the water you drink and, in this case, it is possible that the water comes out again with something you ate the previous day, somewhat as if you were having a stomach wash. Among other things, there can be some sudden and serious intolerance to certain foods that your body will reject instantaneously; conversely, there can be a new fondness for certain foods. Some people might feel the need to reduce their meat consumption. This does not mean that we should not eat meat, since we need a minimum of proteins and nature itself indicated animals to us as a source for this nutrient. It is simply because the fat contained in meat burdens our energy bodies and slows down our metabolism; so during the purification process, there are days when the cleansing energy will reject certain foods that create blockage in order to better circulate. Plants too have souls, although not like humans, and if we were to stop eating meat completely because animals have souls, then we would have to stop killing plants too. In arctic regions, people have no choice but to have a diet almost completely based on meat. Whereas in Amazonia, since people have access to lots of fruits, grains and vegetables, they eat more of these and consume meat in moderation. As in everything, it is an exaggeration that we must avoid the consumption of meat products. Even water, which is indispensable to survival, can expose us to death when we consume too much of it. For people who decide to become vegetarians altogether, there is no obligation to consume meat either as long as the need for proteins is met adequately through plant foods. Jesus said, that it is not what goes into our mouth that defiles us, but what comes out of our mouth. If we were in a different environment, our diet would be different. Here, we can reasonably use what nature is offering us, while being very careful about what we eat because it is very important at the energetic and spiritual levels. It is in the combination of foods that we must be careful and most importantly pay attention to what our body accepts or does not accept. This is something I am learning myself. The Mediterranean diet has been mentioned for several years as a reference when it comes to a healthy diet and it is true that it represents a good example of a balanced food practice in the sense that it consists in consuming a little bit of everything, in moderate quantity. The lion must continue eating antelopes and man must continue eating moderately everything that is edible for there to be balanced. If all regularly consumed species were no longer eaten at all, there will be overpopulation of them at some point and I do not think that the universe intends for us to start castrating the goats and the poultry to prevent their breeding. When our body requires a transition towards a diet purely based on plants that will happen very naturallys because our habitat itself will undergo certain transformations to facilitate our adaptation. We should certainly not force anything; all personal choices are good as long as they suit our needs, do not cause us harm, and as long as we always adopt the path of moderation. I would like to mention that the industrial production of meat is a market with abhorrent practices for animals and humans alike. This is another field that needs reformation. People who have access to farms and local markets are therefore less exposed to the quantity of heavy metals that enter our bodies on a daily basis and contribute to fighting barbarism against animals. On another note, consuming artificial meat produced by 3D printing, like I once heard, can only lead us to some new health issues.

When our organism requires the transition to a purely plant-based diet, it will happen naturally because our habitat itself will undergo certain transformations to facilitate our adaptation. Above all, nothing should be forced; all personal choices are good, as long as they suit our needs, do not harm us, and we always adopt the path of moderation.

SHORT-TERM PHYSICAL DISORIENTATIONS: Sudden episodes of vertigo or dizziness; momentary sense of imbalance; at times problems with diction, difficulty finding one's words or temporary losses of memory.

VARIOUS PAINS AND SYMPTOMS OF SICKNESS: Heart pains and palpitations, hot flushes in the entire body or in specific areas, sensation of wind in the legs, headaches, muscle spasms, pressures in the skull, various bodily pains, sudden goose bumps or chills, frequent cracking of articulations, occasional sensation of a fresh breeze in some parts of the body such as the palms of the hands or the fingertips, the toes, the back and the soles of the feet, the forehead, the legs, etc., are other symptoms of the energy circulating in you and purifying you. Some pains can be excruciating and be concentrated in a specific spot in your body, based on present or past illnesses or wounds, or based on your existential history, that is, your karma. Until my late teens, I suffered from a pain on the left side of my abdomen, for which no medical condition had been detected. It disappeared over time but reappeared with intensity at the beginning of my spiritual ascension. Over a period of three days, it cloistered me at home and I understood that it must be related to some illness or wound in my past life. If in your subconscious, there are some wounds, sorrows, fears, and past relationship conflicts that are not evacuated, all this will create invisible energetic knots that cause blockages in some organs. The powerful spiritual energy that is awakening and trying to move in you will therefore have to force these barriers in order to break them, hence the intensity of the pain. You will really sense it moving through you, focusing on one area at a time. Thus, for several days, you could sense it present in one arm, on a specific spot, then at another moment, it might be in one ear for a few days, then on your skull, and so on and so forth. It can happen that for some time, you feel like there is a bug moving in your ear, in the sole of your feet, in your eyelid, or any other part of your body, creating a sensation of tingling, sometimes of stinging and burning, occasionally of itching. You could also feel and even see carbon evaporating from your body, with the impression of eliminating some "atomic waste". You could have the sensation that a lukewarm liquid substance is circulating in your spine. It is the kundalini arising. Gradually, it will travel through every fibre of your body, changing temperature (sometimes warm, sometimes cold, and sometimes lukewarm) and state (sometimes solid, sometimes liquid, and sometimes gaseous), and you will understand on your own, by the way it works on certain parts of the body, that it is healing you. I encourage you to go to the hospital if you feel unbearable pain and you are not sure that it is related to your spiritual washing. Generally, if it is related to your spiritual awakening, medical exams will reveal no problem.

STRANGE SENSATIONS: Some of them may seem very bizarre, sometimes uncomfortable, especially when you are in public. However, you will have to avoid judging them or overanalysing them. Cooperation being a fundamental condition to help the rise of the sacred fire up to the brain, it is absolutely necessary that you trust God throughout the whole process and that you do not panic about all the things happening in your body. And if the body and the mind are not strengthened by healthy habits, there are risks of complications that could be fatal to physical and mental health.

If it happens that you have the impression that a giant spider has landed on your skull, inserting its legs as fine as needles into your neurons, provoking sensations of stings, burnings or itchings, do not be mistaken about it. It is the divine energy still, for it can take any practical form to work; in this case to proceed with the opening of your crown chakra. At times, you will feel it liquefy and spray tiny water droplets from your skull, or flow inside your body like water. Yet, you will not see this water, even if occasionally, you clearly hear the dull sound of a drop of water falling on your garment or on the floor. The DNA molecule, which contains the program of our biological development, has the aspect of a filament coiled like an electric cable, sometimes partially elongated. It will happen that all day long you have the sensation that literally some threads are uncoiled from the sole of your feet all the way to the top of your skull, then are "rewound", with the impression that an invisible hand is stretching them, and then forming small knots on them. The crown chakra is generally described as a lotus of one thousand petals, and it may feel at some point that indeed petals are growing on the top of your skull. Day after day, the kundalini will transform into a multitude of thin strips, growing in numbers as if someone was braiding your hair. When you are ready to receive the divine anointing, you will literally feel some oil poured onto your head without seeing it and you will feel a very gentle hand laid on you for a while; you will then understand that you are receiving a special grace.

VIBRATORY INTERFERENCE WITH ELECTRONIC DEVICES: I can only talk about this in the simplest way that I have observed the phenomenon. It seems that at times, you release such a strong electric current that you rise from your bed and your own bed sheet projects small lightning flashes; you walk by a lamp and it goes off on its own because of your "high voltage". You touch a computer or any other technological device and it stops functioning for a while, then starts functioning again on its own and sometimes better than before the breakdown (this is not like when there is a system reboot). This type of phenomenon is not frequent, however.

VARIOUS PERCEPTIONS AND SENSITIVITY TO THE VIBRATIONS OF OTHERS: There can be an intermittent buzzing in the ears and a clear perception of God's breath in the silence. A sudden ability to see or feel the aura around people can be born as well. It can happen that while being in public places, your body absorbs some heavy vibrations, as though, due to your enhanced empathy, you were catching some of the emotional baggage in the environment. That will be followed by periods of lethargy during which you feel like your body weighs nearly a ton, succeeded by periods of overflow of energy. The simplest way of living this process, which gradually decreases in intensity, is to just accept the various reactions of your body without judgment or complaint and to adapt to them. It is true that it is not easy at all some days, and in my case, I have noticed that an infusion or a soothing tea helps to soften the effects. The painful stage is very temporary. When it ended for me, I was warned through a dream that the hardest part was over and what was left would be painless. The sensations then became lighter and lighter, and even appeasing at times.

When your spiritual vision improves, it will happen that you see from the corner of your eye some shadows passing day and night. In the deepest stage of sleep during which the soul sometimes reaches the subtle field of existence on which are stored collective memories, that are called akashic records, it will happen that one sees some spirits residing there. You can thus abruptly emerge from a dream to see passing above you, like in a projection of images on a screen, different faces, either appearing in profile or observing you in a non-aggressive way. By the diversity of these apparitions, I instinctively knew that it was not necessarily people that I had personally known who were appearing like that in my room at three or four o'clock in the morning. There have been spirits of both genders, of all races, of all ages. I have seen many people who looked like bearded scholars as people in beautiful period attire or young people in disguise costumes. I have also seen alphabetic letters passing. Some people whose medium abilities are completely developed will perhaps be able to obtain a lot of information from this plane of existence. However, I am not making a confusion between these "images" and the actual visits of beings from another dimension. In this last case, you always feel their real presence and you see their silhouette. As I mentioned earlier, sometimes, after I had a dream conveying an important message, when I wake up, I can see the person or the persons who just communicated with me through a dream. I know that it is a benevolent presence by the calm way in which they signal their presence so that I know that the message is authentic, before disappearing. One afternoon, I wept desperately after thinking about some injustices. That same night, I dreamed a dream whose meaning was that there is still hope. When I opened my eyes and saw in a blurry way, the person who just restored my courage in that manner, I was deeply moved and I mentally thanked him warmly. A benevolent presence is never intrusive, the reason why it signals itself softly, moves with grace and exudes serenity. It even happens that a benevolent spirit surrounds themself with an ethereal light so that you can see them if the room is too dark. On the contrary, a malevolent presence is aggressive, announces itself noisily sometimes, wants to create fear in you, or tries to distract you. But in general, as long as you do not know exactly what type of spirit is visiting you, you should avoid looking a spiritual entity straight in the eyes because it is through the eyes that a soul can be hypnotised. If the entity itself tries insistently to catch your gaze, look away and only look at them in profile. You can also start seeing very distinctively with your naked eye or through meditation the double of yourself that is called the Higher Self, that is, our body dwelling in the soul, the divine entity within us. It is him the small inner voice. Our communications with this divine part of us become increasingly clear as we progress. Personally, my Higher Self appears to me at any time of the day or night.

UNIFICATION OF THE TWO HEMISPHERES OF THE BRAIN: The brain is the most complex computer system in existence. As a first step during the spiritual ascension, it is reprogrammed in a way to remove all the things blocking access to a higher dimension of consciousness. Thus, even with a brain with two hemispheres (left and right) as the majority of us have, one no longer perceives reality in the same way, for one gets out of the duality paradigm (separation from one another), and integrates in a balanced, harmonious way, both the female energy (deriving from earth) and the male energy (deriving from heaven). You fully embrace your identity, either male or female, and you perceive both genders are complementary and not opposed, with a feeling of unity with all that exists. Many people are being born already transformed that way by past experiences or are reaching this new state during their lifetime through the learning of lessons.

The next step is the morphological unification of the two hemispheres to form a complete brain. This is what allows us to transition into a consciousness of the fifth dimension and reconnection with the Higher Self, increasing spiritual capacities such as intuition, telepathic sensibility, and clairvoyance. I did not need any explanation to understand what was happening in my brain when it started the "closing" of the slit separating the two sides. Over several days, I tangibly felt the sacred fire weaving fibres between the left side and the right side, from the base of the skull on the neck level, all the way to the top. A few days before the beginning of this phase, I was warned through flies. Sometimes, we receive messages through animals. When I got home one evening, I was surprised to see a swarm of flies on the window of my apartment's back door, something that never happened in four summers spent at the same place, while I had not even opened that door at all that day. And the most interesting thing was that they were tranquilly stuck to the glass on the inside. Although intrigued, I kindly escorted the undesirable visitors outside. Since their number practically doubled the following afternoon, on the same spot, I made sure that my trash can was not the cause of this sudden invasion and that there were no cracks around my doors and windows. I also verified that there was no food residue on the balcony and clogged an interstice with a cloth. Yet, they reappeared mysteriously that same evening. I then told myself that maybe they were not there for the sheer pleasure of annoying me and I decided to leave them there for the night since they were not making any noise. Then I started reading about the symbolism of a fly. In fact, they invade in large numbers decaying food, a sign that something is dead or is dying. Therefore, I understood that I was being prompted to make some change or that some change was being announced. Feeling intuitive that the time had come for me to move on to something else, I had just resigned from my job a few days before with no guarantee of something else to ensure the payment of my bills. I had simply resolved to step back a little and was determined to quickly find another occupation, and I actually took a temporary job a few days after I left the work. Thus, I first thought that these insects simply came to confirm that I had made the right choice. Indeed, as soon as I understood that they came to notify me of some change, they disappeared. And it was on the following day that the unification of both sides of my brain started. I realised that they appeared when the old version of me was symbolically decaying, in a way.

After one week of this transformation work, I dreamed a dream that was as clear as daylight. I saw myself in the evening in a big market, looking for my way. As I was walking, I remembered one entrance to the market's main building, which opens onto a small aisle. When I found that entrance, I asked for directions from a few shopkeepers inside, and following the indications, I came to the new house that my sister was occupying with her family. As I was asking her young cleaning lady if they were satisfied with the new toilets, the bathroom door opened a little and I saw a newborn lying on his back wrapped up in a white linen as if he had just been bathed and delicately placed there. This newborn had a firm body and mature features as if he was an adult, and it was at that moment that I woke from sleep. Interpretation: the market is a place of communication and exchange which in a dream symbolises life or the world, depending on the contexts; the baby symbolises an inner birth or a new beginning; the white linen symbolises the original state of innocence and unity. It thus clearly appeared to me that after looking for my way in the animated market of life, I came back home, to a family, in a reality of non-separation; in short, I was accessing a higher dimension of consciousness, thus that I was being born again, as the flies had announced. Ever since, I feel light moving through my organs with much fluidity and my ascension continues with great delicacy.

ACTIVATION OF SPECIAL GIFTS OR ABILITIES, REINFORCED PROTECTION: The goal of this ascension is to make you reach a state of clairvoyance and allow you to access the ancient knowledge imprinted in your genes. Never again will you doubt the existence of a supreme being and the possibility that life exists outside of this planet. Your intuitive abilities will increase tenfold, but you should not expect to develop some superpowers overnight; the gifts that we receive depend on the abilities that are dormant in us and will increase over time based on our progress. Let us pay attention to the fact that to start in a state of pure energy and then reach this physical form that moves, thinks, and feels is already something magical. As for the gifts that will be added through progress in consciousness, everything will depend on the reprogramming of your DNA, which is always linked to the stage your soul has reached on its path. Thus, it will not be given to someone something the person is not ready to handle so as not to disturb his or her evolution. There is no anarchy or injustice in God. What is certain is that, regardless of the level of progress of each person, the ascension will bring you physical, emotional, and psychological healing, and will ensure you a natural reinforced protection. Do not forget that you must be willing to attract it. And this willingness must absolutely be selfless. In the way that we currently function on this planet, almost everything is motivated by calculation, by satisfaction of personal interest. Yet, we receive enormously from the universe whose foundation is selfless love. If therefore your willingness to rediscover it is not nurtured by healthy curiosity, but rather by the sole desire of taking advantage of it, there is little chance that the universe will come closer to you.

End Word

At every cycle of rebirth, our past life memories are erased; some people will be able to recover them. Just like for the planet, there is around our body an electromagnetic field of protection known to ancient civilizations. It will be activated through your determination to choose goodness only, even if that entails some difficult choices. Not only it is the vehicle that will facilitate the continuation of your ascension towards a higher dimension of consciousness, but once it is deployed, it will be much more difficult for anyone to cause you harm gratuitously as long as your heart remains pure. If an entity or a person harms you unfairly, the rebound effect will be faster and more devastating. The karmic chaining of the aggressor becomes more powerful and the *reimbursement* of the debt is accelerated. Why is it activated through healthy behaviour and a personality oriented towards love and faith? Because it contains God's spirit and the Creator has engineered it that way so that the real evolution of man is linked to his consciousness and not just the mastering of the physical world. Our level of conscience is what puts us on top of the animal kingdom, it is only natural that its development is the measure of our progress. It cannot be otherwise.

Love and peace be with you all.

Made in the USA
Monee, IL
03 May 2026